JI

THE CHILD'S GUIDE TO HEAVEN

JESUS THE WAY

OR,

THE CHILD'S GUIDE TO HEAVEN

BY REV. EDWARD PAYSON HAMMOND, M. A.

Solid Ground Christian Books
2090 Columbiana Rd, Suite 2000
Birmingham, AL 35216
205-443-0311
sgcb@charter.net
http://solid-ground-books.com

JESUS THE WAY
The Child's Guide to Heaven

Edward Payson Hammond (1831-1910)

Jesus the Way was first published by American Baptist Publication Society

Solid Ground Classic Reprints

First printing of new edition December 2005

Cover work by Borgo Design, Tuscaloosa, AL
Contact them at nelbrown@comcast.net

Special thanks to Ric Ergenbright for permission to use the image on the cover. Visit him at ricergenbright.org

ISBN: 1-59925-035-7

Introduction to New Edition

Edward Payson Hammond spent most of his life seeking to speak to children about his Lord and Savior Jesus Christ. The book you hold in your hands is one of the most precious of his more than 100 books and tracts. What is so special about this book? Let me try to explain:

First, this book is special because from the very first page the author speaks directly to the mind and the heart of children. Rev. Hammond knew children and understood how to speak and write that they would listen, and listen with both ears. There is a directness about each line that causes the reader to feel as if he is the only one in the world the writer has in mind. This makes it very special.

Next, this book is special because it is a book that takes the matters of sin and salvation very seriously. Too often in books for children in our day the subject of sin and salvation is almost ignored. Modern writers seem to feel that you cannot say too much about sin because it would turn away today's child. Rev. Hammond believed with all his heart what the Bible says about children being born in sin, and thus he is always very bold to let children know their greatest need is to repent. This also makes it very special.

Again, this book is special because it is a book that takes the matter of conversion very seriously. The first four chapters are all written to seek to bring children to a knowledge of salvation. He seeks to urge the reader to cry out to the Lord for a new heart that will love God and keep His commandments, and hate the sin formerly loved. Each chapter ends with a pointed prayer the child is urged to use as a model to seek forgiveness from all his sins. These prayers are not to be confused with the "Sinner's Prayer" that has been a plague to the church and the world of the last two centuries. These prayers of Rev. Hammond are not treated like "magic words" that instantly guarantee the salvation of all who utter them. Rather, they are intended as suggestions and models that are to be thought over and used to guide the child as he seeks to pour the heart out to God.

Once again, this book is special because it is filled with Scripture language and Scripture examples. Rev. Hammond believed that *"Faith comes by hearing, and hearing by the Word of God."* He also believed that *"God's Word will not return unto Him void, but will accomplish that which He pleases, and shall prosper in the thing unto which He sent it."* The reader is left with no doubt about the truth of God's Word, found in the 66 Books of the Bible.

Finally, this book is special because it exalts the Lord Jesus Christ to His rightful place. Rev. Hammond had tasted and seen that the Lord is gracious, and he felt compelled to lead others, especially children, to place all their trust in Him as *the only Savior for sinners*. Sadly in our day there are people who teach that Jesus is not the only sure guide to heaven. If you read this book with an open heart you will see that nothing could be further from the truth. To say that anyone can reach heaven who does not come to know, trust and love Jesus is a lie. Our dear friend, Rev. Hammond will make this very clear.

Therefore, in light of these five things, you are invited to read this book with a sincere desire to sit at the feet of Jesus and learn of Him. He alone is THE CHILD'S GUIDE TO HEAVEN. If the Lord is gracious to you and opens your heart to trust in the only Savior of sinners we would love to hear from you, especially if He is pleased to use this book to help you. May all who read these pages be blessed both now and forever!

Michael Gaydosh
Solid Ground Christian Books

CONTENTS

CHAPTER I.

BEYROUT.

PAGE.

In a strange place—The story of how we came there—Why we were kept there—"Guardianos"—Amusing scene—The Holy Land—Application—Jesus the only Way to Heaven—Ready to save little children—Child's Prayer—Poetry. 7

CHAPTER II.

MOUNT LEBANON.

Children's meetings at Beyrout, Syria—Story of two children lost on Mount Lebanon—Forgiveness—Jesus suffering for us—God forgives us for his sake—Child's prayer. 22

CHAPTER III.

DAMASCUS.

A visit to Damascus—Ruins of Naaman's House—The lepers—Tent life—Sarepta—The widow's son raised to

CONTENTS.

PAGE

life—Elijah—Jesus' death for us—Three letters from children—Child saved in "the cleft of the rock"—Jesus "The Child's Guide." 38

CHAPTER IV.

TO JERUSALEM.

Our journey through Palestine—Children's meetings—Sea of Galilee—Poetry—First view of Jerusalem—"Place where he was crucified"—The boy in prayer—Lines, "Jesus Lifted Up"—Short history of life and death of Jesus—Way of salvation—Our feelings in Gethsemane—Story of a soldier who died for his friend—Why God can save us for Jesus' sake—"Soul" sorrow—Poetry, "My New Birthday"—Letter from a boy seven years old—"I felt my weight of sin was gone"—Come to Jesus—Child's prayer—Poetry. 53

CHAPTER V.

VISIT TO CAPERNAUM.

For little Christians—The mother of the Wesleys—Few books for little Christians—A visit to Capernaum—Story of Jairus's daughter—Her love to Jesus—Application—"So wicked not to love Jesus"—Five links of the golden chain—Child's prayer answered—Work for Jesus. 85

JESUS THE WAY

CHAPTER I.

BEYROUT.

I THINK no one ever began to write a book for children in such a place as I am in now. I will not tell you at present the name of the place where I am, but will describe it to you, and then see if *you*, my little friend, can tell yourself.

If you were to look at the high walls all around us, and at the strong grating of our windows, and then at the guards that keep close watch over us all day, and sleep at each of our doors on the ground at night, you would think that we were surely in prison. And then, if you should see how no one is allowed to touch us, except those who came in the same ship with us; and how, when the missionaries, Mr. Bliss and Mr. Jessup, came to see us, they were not allowed to shake hands with us, but were kept a long way from us by a guard with a long stick,— you would think it must be that we all had the leprosy, such as those ten men had, who, when they came to Jesus, "stood afar off, and lifted up their voices, and said, Jesus, Master, have mercy on us" (Luke xvii. 12, 13).

Let me tell you the way we were treated, when we landed in this harbor of Beyrout.

We had a good many friends in the city, and of course we wanted to go ashore at once, and commence our journey on horseback through Palestine. But the officers of the Turkish government wanted to make a little money, and would not let us do that.

Pretty soon a boat came alongside, and some one called my name. Down the long ship-stairs I hurried to the side of the ship; but, instead of handing the letter to me, they pushed off as if I was some monster ready to kill them, and they took a long board, and laid a letter on it, and handed it to me. This letter was from a gentleman whom I knew six years ago in Scotland, and who wanted to see me; but when I made a motion to the Turks in the boat that they should take me in their boat to the shore, they seemed frightened at the thought. We then wrote a line on a card and threw it into the boat for them to take on shore. If a bombshell had fallen among them, they could not have been more frightened. They all lifted up their hands and began to gesticulate, as if we had done something dreadful. Not one of them dared to touch the card. After talking a long time with great seriousness, they appointed one of their number to take a knife, about a foot long, and pierce it. This he did in a sort of way that looked as if he was killing some deadly viper. Then he laid it over the edge of the boat till a curious-looking basket was brought, and then our clean card was put into it, as if it was a serpent that was ready to bite them all. We found out afterward that, because this card had been in our hands, it had to be "smoked" before it could be given to our friend.

We were then told that we could not go to the city of Beyrout, but that there was a place for us half a mile beyond the city, where we must stop a while. So we had to get into a boat, and then some other men in another boat took hold of a long rope, and towed our boat to the place where we now are. The men in the boat who had been pulling us toward our prison-house seemed so much afraid to touch us, we wondered how they would dare to take their pay from us. But they contrived a way which made us laugh most heartily. One of the men pulled off his clothes just as we drew near the shore, and, taking an earthen dish in his hand, swam to the side of our boat and called for *baksheesh*. So we each dropped the money into his stone money-purse, and it was then sent off to be "smoked" before they dared to touch it. For they knew if they took anything from us, that they would have to go into the same place where we were going. As soon as these men left us, a great Turk came and showed us our rooms, and appointed for each of us a *guardiano*, who was seriously told that he must not leave us, night or day. And so at night, while one lies down on the ground outside of our door to sleep, the other walks up and down, to see that we make no attempt to escape.

There are about three hundred here. We are not kept in our rooms, except at night. In the daytime we can go about the large grounds anywhere inside of the walls; and as we are on the sea-shore, we can bathe just when we like. We sent off to a hotel and got some good, clean furniture for our room, and every day we have the best of food brought to us. Some nice Christian people from America are with us, and all who visit Palestine must stop in this place for ten days. It would make you laugh to see us led about by our Turkish guards. When the missionaries came to see us, one of them was almost ready to shake hands with us, but our guard pointed to us with a look of horror, and cried, "Unclean! unclean!" Yes, if they had touched us, they would have had to be put in here for ten days.

It makes no difference who comes to this port from certain places, they must be put for a while in this prison. There are two consuls here now. Rev. Dr. Patton, of Chicago, has to make it his home. Little children are here. A few nights ago, a man gave his guard about a hundred dollars to let him escape, and in the middle of the night, away he fled to Mount Lebanon. If he is found, we are told that he will be shot.

I think by this time you must know what sort of a place we are in. Yes, it is quarantine. This place is more often called a *lazaretto*. There was no cholera on board our ship, but the Turkish government has made a law that all who come here from certain cities shall suffer ten days' quarantine; and as we came from Alexandria, in Egypt, we have had to be shut up here. We have had plenty of books and good company, and good surf-bathing, and it has been a good rest for us; yet, after all, we have been impatient to get on our way to Damascus and Jerusalem, and to some of the many other places of which we read in the Bible.

In America, if there is cholera on board a ship from England, our officers keep it from coming into the harbor for a while; but other ships, that have what they call "a clean bill of health," they let come directly in. And so we thought, as there was not one sick on our ship, we might have been permitted to come at once into Beyrout. But the law was against us, and so here we have been confined.

Now, my dear children, why do you think I have been so careful to tell about our quarantine prison? It has been that I might teach you an important lesson. We tried a long time, and spent a good deal of money, to get into Jerusalem without having to be put in quarantine. If we had not been careful, we should have been in two or three other lazarettos, before we reached this one.

Now, the Bible, you know, tells us about the "New Jerusalem." You all want to go there. But you can never get there till you are first made clean in the blood of "the Lamb that was slain." Though our guards often cried out, "Unclean! unclean! don't touch the Americans!" when any one was ready to touch us, yet we knew that it was all imagination, and that we were a great deal cleaner than all our Turkish guards. None of us had the cholera, but each of us was in perfect health. But you, my dear child, however young you are, if you are not a Christian, you are unclean in the sight of God. Every sin you have ever committed has left a dark stain upon your soul. If you could find any way to get into heaven as you are now, all covered with the leprosy of sin, none of the angels would touch you. I think they would be more afraid of you than these Turks were of us. They would not let you stay there at all. God would tell them to take you off into some sort of a quarantine. Perhaps you would hear from the lips of the Great King those words in Matthew xxii. 13: "Bind him hand and foot, and take him away, and cast him into outer darkness; there shall be weeping and gnashing of teeth." These are dreadful words, and I hope and pray that you may never hear them spoken to you.

Whenever you are called to die, you want to go at once to Jesus, don't you? "Oh, yes!" I hear you say. But are you sure that, if you were to die, even now, you would go there? You have a disease worse than the cholera—you are sin-sick. Yes, you are a leprous sinner, and God will never let you into heaven till you are made white and clean. You may be more anxious to go to the beautiful New Jerusalem above than we were to get to the Jerusalem where Jesus was crucified; but you will never get there till your guilty stains are washed away.

We wanted very much to get to this Holy Land where the Bible was written, and where the apostles and prophets lived and died; but we spent weeks and a great deal of money trying to get rid of the quarantines which were in our way; and though we did avoid some, yet we could not escape this one. Just so, a good many young people want to go, when they die, to the heavenly Canaan; but they think being a Christian here on earth is much like getting into quarantine—that the only object of becoming a Christian is just to get ready for heaven. But this is a great mistake.

We have to stay here eight days, and two days on board ship, to fill up the ten days' quarantine. Some of the children cry, and want to get out very much. But it will not take you as many days to come to Jesus, who died on the cross for you. He will take you the moment you come to him. He loves to receive little children, and wash their sins all away, and make them fit for the New Jerusalem above. And, once more, when you have become a Christian, you will find yourself far happier than you ever were before. You will only be sorry that you did not come sooner. You will, like that poor leper in

Luke xvii. 15, feel like falling down before Jesus, and "giving him thanks."

If we should run out of this quarantine before they think us "clean" from all taint of cholera, they would shoot us; but our time is up to-morrow, and then we can take our horses and flee away to the side of Mount Lebanon, whose snowy top, nine thousand feet high, we have spent hours in looking at from our prison house. But if you will only trust in the Saviour who loves you so much, you can in due time enter heaven, and there they will love to receive you. Now, if you want to know how to get through the quarantine that will fit you for a happier life here and hereafter, you will find two verses which will tell you. "*If we confess our sins, he is faithful and just to forgive us our sins, and to cleanse us from all unrighteousness*" (1 John i. 9). "BELIEVE ON THE LORD JESUS CHRIST, AND THOU SHALT BE SAVED" (Acts xvi. 31).

JESUS THE WAY.

Yes, my little friend, the only way to get to heaven is to come as a poor lost sinner to Christ. He has bled and died on the cross, that you might be forgiven. If you will come to him and trust him, you will find his heart full of love to you. Yes, he loves to save little children. He will give you a new heart, so that you will love good things and hate bad things, if you will come and ask him for it.

I have known many little children who were taught by God how to trust in Jesus when they came to him with a prayer like the following upon their lips. Try and make this prayer your own; ask God to help you to feel every word of it, and you too may learn what Jesus means when he says, "I AM THE WAY," and you will find JESUS to be "THE CHILD'S GUIDE TO HEAVEN."

CHILD'S PRAYER.

O God, I am a sinful child. I wish to get

to heaven, but I am covered with sin. As I am now, I am not fit for heaven. The leprosy of sin is upon my soul. But in thy word thou hast told me that "the blood of Jesus Christ thy Son cleanseth from all sin," and that he has been "wounded for our transgressions," and that "if we confess our sins, thou art faithful and just to forgive us our sins, and to cleanse us from all unrighteousness." O God, I confess my sins. I have not loved thee; I have not loved thy word; I have not obeyed thy laws; I have not loved thy dear Son, who died on the cross that I might be forgiven and be made ready for heaven. I know I cannot get to heaven except through Christ. Lord, help me to believe in him and love him. This I ask for Jesus' sake. Amen.

> Although a child, I've often sought,
> To know the way to heaven;
> Of Jesus I have long been taught,
> But never been forgiven.

JESUS THE WAY.

With sorrow deep I've ne'er confessed
  How wicked I have been;
But look, O Lord, within my breast,
  And teach me all my sin.

And help me, Lord, with grief heart-felt,
  To sorrow for my guilt;
Dear Jesus, cause my heart to melt,—
  For me thy blood was spilt.

Thou art the only quarantine
  Between this earth and heaven
And all who there would e'er be seen,
  By thee must be forgiven.

Dear Saviour, now to thee I come,—
  To thee alone I cling,
Oh, take me to thy glorious home,
  And then thy praise I'll sing.

CHAPTER II.

MOUNT LEBANON.

I WANT to tell you, my little friend, what we did after we came out of quarantine,—of which I told you in the last chapter.

Within an hour from the time we left that gloomy place, we were in a nice chapel, or church, as they called it, standing before about three hundred children and youth.

Rev. Dr. Jessup, one of the American missionaries, had asked me to talk to these children, and to tell them about the little ones, in the United States, who had learned to love the dear Saviour.

I thought I had never seen such queer looking children. Each of the girls wore a white lace *mandilla*, like a veil, over her head; and the boys each a red Turkish *fez*, or cap. With their sparkling, black eyes, they looked really beautiful.

I could not speak Arabic, and so the Rev. Dr. Jessup translated what was said. They seemed quite surprised that we had come so far away from America to see the land where the Bible was written, and where our dear Saviour died for us on the cross.

It was a great joy for us to see those dear children gathered in that nice building. They all seemed eager to hear about Jesus, —"THE CHILD'S GUIDE TO HEAVEN."

That sight made me feel very thankful to God that he had put it into the hearts of Christians in America to send good men away five thousand miles to Beyrout, to teach poor heathen about the way to get to heaven.

I should like to tell you of the children's meetings, which we held in that city of eighty-five thousand people, and of some of those dear children who, I think, gave their hearts to Jesus; but I must tell you now of two little ones who attended those meetings. This little story will help you to understand something very important, which I wish to teach you.

One day when I was in Mrs. Thompson's school, she called two little ones to her, and asked me to notice them, for she said she wished to tell me a story about them. One was about eight, and another ten years of age. I think you will like to hear this story, and so I shall now tell it to you.

These children's parents lived on the side of Mount Lebanon, several miles from Beyrout. And when they heard of Mrs. Thompson's school, and that she was willing to take their children, and feed them, and clothe them, and educate them, they took them away down the mountain-side, and gave them into her care. After a while, one morning, one of these children said to the other, "I want to go home and see father and mother."

"Well, let us go after breakfast."

"But it is so far, how can we ever find the way?"

"No matter, we will try; we won't stay here."

So, after breakfast, they stole out of the yard by the back gate, and off they went, trying to find their way home; but they soon got lost.

When Mrs. Thompson found that the children were gone, she was very much frightened. She did not know but that some wicked person had stolen them away. She got all she could to help her find them. For a long, long time they looked about in all directions, but could not find them. Some were sent away to the lofty sides of Mount

Lebanon, where their home had been; but they were not there. Then their father and mother began to look about for them, but they could not find any trace of them.

At last, after a great deal of trouble, the children were found, and brought back to Mrs. Thompson's school. Their father was present at the time.

He said to Mrs. Thompson, "You must punish these children very hard. Don't spare them, no matter how much they cry. They have been so ungrateful for all your kindness. Whip them; whip them."

The poor little things wept very much, for they expected no mercy.

Mrs. Thompson called them up before the whole school, and spoke of what a wicked thing they had done, to run away from such a good school. The scholars all felt that they deserved to be punished. But Mrs. Thompson was a very kind-hearted woman, and so she said to the children, "It would be quite right for me to punish you. But, instead of punishing you this time, I will forgive you, if you will confess how naughty you have been."

They said they were sorry, and would never run away again; and so they were freely forgiven.

Then their tears were wiped away, and Mrs. Thompson smiled upon them. She treated them afterwards just as if they had not disobeyed her and run away from her school. Do you wonder that they loved her for her kindness to them? What would you have thought of them if they had never once thanked her, and what should she have done to them if they had run away again, and aroused all the neighbors? You know Mrs. Thompson was not paid for teaching them. It was all because she loved them, and wished to have them learn to trust in Jesus, that she took them from their mountain home to her nice school. But suppose that in many ways they had disobeyed her, and though she fed and clothed them, treated her as if they tried to forget her, as if they did not love to think about her. Would you not say they deserved a good whipping?

I think I hear you say, "I know if any one had taken me from a heathen home to some nice school, and fed and clothed me, I would not have been so ungrateful."

But, my dear child, I know of something worse than that which *you* have done. I know of some One who has done a thousand times more for you than that kind lady did for those two children, and yet you have run away from him. You have disobeyed him; you have tried to forget all about him. All that he asks of you, for his great kindness, is that you should love him, and obey his good laws. But you have many times rejected him. Yes, and I must tell you, though you will scarcely believe me, you have *hated* him.

But you say, "Why, you are talking to me as if I was a heathen? I have not been so bad as all that. I try to be a good child; I say my prayers; I read my Bible; I try to do right; I often think about heaven, for I want to go there when I die."

I believe all you say, and yet if you are not a true Christian, what I say is true too.

If you have not come to Jesus, had your *sins all forgiven*, and a *new heart* given to you, then you are an enemy of Christ; for he says, "HE THAT IS NOT WITH ME IS AGAINST ME." And, in Isaiah, he says, "All we like sheep have gone astray" (Isa. liii. 6). Yes, we are all prodigals. You have read, in the fifteenth chapter of Luke, that beautiful story which Jesus told about the prodigal son, who left his good father's house, and because he was so proud and wicked, "gathered all together and took his journey into a far country, and there wasted his substance with riotous living."

Ah! my child, if you will read that story carefully, you will see a picture of yourself in it. Young as you are, *you* are the prodigal that Jesus was talking about. You have gone away from your heavenly Father, who has given you every good thing you ever had. He has been far kinder to you than Mrs. Thompson was to those two little girls; and for all his goodness to you he has said often to you, "Give me thine heart,—love me." But if you are not a Christian you have not loved him at all. You have not heeded his words. And he says, "He that loveth me not, keepeth not my sayings." And again, "He that hath my commandments and keepeth them, he it is that loveth me" (John xiv. 21–24).

Now you know you have not always done right; your conscience tells you so. Have you not been angry many times, and spoken naughty words? Jesus says, "He that is angry with his brother without a cause, shall be in danger of the judgment."

Did you ever tell a lie? *Ah, then, you are a lost sinner,* and if you should die this moment, without repentance, you would never get to heaven. Just open your Bible at Revelation xxi. 8, and see what awful words are spoken about liars.

Now the question comes, Can God forgive you as Mrs. Thompson forgave those two children?

You said that if they had not been sorry for disobeying her, but had run away again, they ought to have been punished. But you have disobeyed God many times, and, like the prodigal, have been living in "a far country," feeding on "husks." How then can he forgive you? I know he wishes to do this for you. He loves you far more than that lady loved those dear children.

I will try and answer this important question for you. God in mercy has contrived a wonderful plan by which he can "BE JUST AND THE JUSTIFIER OF HIM THAT BELIEVETH IN JESUS."

He has found One mighty to save (Isa. lxiii. 1). Yes, "God so loved the world that he gave his only begotten Son, that whosoever believeth in him should not perish, but have everlasting life" (John iii. 16). Oh, how kind it was in his dear Son to be willing to die for us!

> "Which of all our friends to save us,
>   Could or would have shed his blood?
> But this Jesus died to have us
>   Reconciled in him to God."

If some one of the scholars in that school had said to their teacher,—"I love those girls that have run away. I know they deserve to be punished for their disobedience. I fear they will be afraid to come back, for they will expect to be punished. Now let me be punished in their stead. Let me suffer just what they deserve; and then let me go and find them, and tell them that I have taken their place, and that you, for my sake, are ready to forgive them." And suppose that scholar had really taken the chastisement which the others deserved, and then had gone out and found them away on the mountain-side, and after telling them all about it, had said, "Come back; Mrs. Thompson will now forgive you for my sake. Here is a letter from her in which she says so." Do you not think they would be quite willing to go back to the school? "Oh yes," you say, "I am sure they would." But Jesus comes to you with a more touching story than that. Yes, "the Son of man is come to seek and to save that which was lost." You are the lost one he has come to seek and to save. He says to you, "I have suffered on the cross that you might be forgiven. See where the crown of thorns was pressed down upon my brow for you. See the 'prints of the nails' in my hands. I was scourged with a great whip, in Pilate's hall, until the blood ran down my back. I was buffeted and spit upon. I have been wounded for thy transgressions. I have been bruised for thy iniquities. I have borne thy sins in mine own body on the tree. God, who is displeased with thee for all thy guilt, is now ready to forgive thee for my sake. Come with me, and I will ask him for my sake to pardon thee. Come and tell him you are sorry, and he will, he will forgive you. I have suffered for thy sins, 'the just for the unjust, that I might bring thee to God.'"

Oh, my dear little friend, can you reject such a Saviour? He is the "CHILD'S GUIDE TO HEAVEN." Trust in him, and for his sake your sins will all be pardoned. Will you not turn to him at once? and with these words upon your lips, and with your little hand in the Saviour's, come like the prodigal to your heavenly Father with this

PRAYER.

Father, I have sinned against heaven, and in thy sight, and am no more worthy to be called thy son. I have wandered far away from thee. I have often disobeyed thee. I have not loved thee. When I have done wrong I have tried to forget thee. I have lived "without God, and without hope in the world." Thou mightest have driven me away from thy presence for ever. But this my dear Saviour, thy Son, has taken my place. "He was wounded for our transgressions, and bruised for our iniquities." He has shown me where the nails pierced his hands, and made them fast to the cross. He has opened my blind eyes to see himself as *my* Redeemer, who paid the debt for me; "who his own self bare our sins in his own body on the tree." O God, forgive me, for Jesus' sake, and by thy Holy Spirit give me a new heart. Hear this, my prayer, only for Jesus' sake. Amen.

I have written below a little prayer for you, which you may like to learn.

CHILD'S PRAYER.

Heavenly Father, pity me,
　For my soul is full of sin;
I have wandered far from thee,
　Oh, how wicked I have been!
Can I ever be forgiven?
　Can my sins be washed away
So that I shall sing in heaven,
　Where from thee no children stray.

Canst thou love a wicked child,
　Who has often disobeyed?
Canst thou ever on me smile,
　As if from thee I'd not strayed?
Those poor heathen little ones
　Only once ran from their school,
But alas! how many times
　I have broken from thy rule.

Dearest Father, speak to me
　As thou didst to Samuel;
I can only come to thee,
　Thou alone my fears canst quell.
Oft thy voice to me has called,
　But I did not listen then;
Surely I will hearken now,
　If thou wilt but speak again.

ANSWER.

Yes, my child, 'tis thee I love,
    Though thou art so full of guilt;
My dear Son came from above
    And for thee his blood has spilt.
All thy sins on him were laid,
    When he suffered on the tree;
He the dreadful debt has paid;
    Trust in him, and thou art free.

Now the wicked I forgive,
    When in Jesus' name they pray;
Such with me in heaven shall live
    And be happy there for aye.
Come to me, then, little one,
    I will change thy wicked heart;
Only trust in my dear Son,
    Never, never, from him part

CHAPTER III.

DAMASCUS.

AS I have told you a little about our stay in quarantine, and our visit to Beyrout, in Syria, you may be interested in following us a little further in the land of the Bible.

We first went over the great Mount Lebanon and Anti-Lebanon on our way to Damascus. When we reached that most ancient city in the world, we walked through "the street which is called Straight," along which blind Saul of Tarsus was led to the house of Judas. There we saw queer looking baker's shops, and many queer looking places.

Jesus the Way.

DAMASCUS.

We were much interested in seeing what we were told were the ruins of the house of Naaman the leper. We had our Bibles with us, and read the fifth chapter of II. Kings, telling us how a little girl was the means of saving the life of Naaman.

The grounds are now used as a lazar-house, and there we saw nine lepers. Some had lost their hands, others their feet. 'T was a dreadful sight. If there were no sin in the world, there would be no such sad sights as those poor lepers. And we thought of how every sinner was more loathsome in God's sight, than those lepers were to us. Every one, young and old, who has not been washed in Jesus' blood, is a leprous sinner still. And as those lepers were shut up in the lazar-house, so those who, as leprous sinners, come up to the judgment-seat, in the last day, will be shut up in God's lazar-house forever. You can read about that great last day in Matthew xxv.

After seeing Kaukab, the place about ten miles south of Damascus, where, it is supposed, Paul was struck down (Acts ix. 3, 5), we left the many interesting sights in and about Damascus, and returned to Beyrout. There we took horses for a journey through Palestine. Though there were but four in our party, we had fourteen horses besides our own, to carry the men and things we needed during our *tent-life* of thirty days in a country where there are no hotels, except in Jerusalem.

Large tents, beds, tables, trunks, books, and a number of other things, all had to be strapped on the backs of mules and horses. There are not many carriages or wagons in Palestine.

Though it was the middle of November, the weather was very warm and pleasant.

We had nice horses to ride, good food to eat, and something new and interesting to see every day.

The second day we were in our saddles, we came to Sarepta. We turned to I. Kings xvii., and read of how Elijah came there when the place was called Zarephath, and of how every day for a "full year" the Lord fed him, so that he could say, "The barrel of meal wasted not, neither did the cruse of oil fail, according to the word of the Lord." And we read, while in Sarepta, of how the son of the good woman, in whose house he dwelt, "fell sick," and died; of how Elijah "cried unto the Lord for him," and said, "I pray thee let this child's soul come again unto him." "And the Lord heard the voice of Elijah, and the soul of the child came unto him again, and he revived."

We thought of how that child must have felt toward Elijah somewhat as little children feel towards the dear Saviour, who has raised them to a new spiritual life. But I am sure he did not love Elijah half as much as such children love Jesus. All that Elijah did for that son was to pray for him. But Jesus had to *die* for us, and to "bear our sins in his own body on the tree," before he could ask God, for his sake, to save us, and fit us for heaven.

Suppose that when that son lay there sick, some of the wandering Moabites had come to the house of his widowed mother, and threatened to kill him, and that Elijah had offered himself to them, saying, "Let me die in his stead;" and suppose that he had really died to save the life of that boy, would he not have loved the prophet far more than he did after he was raised to life? He would often have said, "How much I owe to that good prophet who *died* to save my life!"

But Jesus has died to save your *soul*. God's words are, "The soul that sinneth, it shall die;" that is, shall be shut out of heaven, and punished forever. Then Jesus said, "Father, let me die for those lost ones." God in mercy accepted the sacrifice. In due time Christ came into this world, and died a dreadful death, on the cross, for our sins; and now God, for Jesus' sake, can forgive us. Oh, how wonderful that Jesus should have died for his *enemies!* Only a few of all who have ever lived have been willing to die for their *friends*, but Jesus died for his *enemies*. Paul says, "When we were enemies, we were reconciled to God by the death of his Son." "God commendeth his love toward us, in that, while we were yet sinners, Christ died for us." (Rom. v. 8-10).

What a great heart of love the dear Saviour must have had, to have been willing to die such a dreadful death for us! What a hard-hearted sinner you must be, if you do not wish to love him.

Here are some lines which I think a little boy in London gave me last summer. I hope you will heed them.

"Here's a message of love
Come down from above,

To invite ltttle children to heaven;
In God's blessed book
Poor sinners may look
And see how all sins are forgiven.

For there they may read
How Jesus did bleed
And die for his dear little ones!
How clean he first makes them,
And afterwards takes them
To be his own daughters and sons.

And oh, when they die,
He takes them on high,
To be with him in heaven above;
For so kind is his heart
That he never will part
From a child that has tasted his love.

Below is a letter from a child in London. She is only eleven years of age, but I think she loves Jesus more than the son of that widow loved Elijah. It would be strange if she did not. She says, "I HAVE GIVEN MY HEART TO JESUS, AND I FEEL HAPPIER THAN I EVER DID BEFORE."

"DEAR MR. HAMMOND,—I am ry pleased to tell you that I have giv y heart to Jesus, and feel happier than I ever did before. I pray every morning and evening to Jesus to keep me in the right road. I have a great many trials, and am very often tempted to do things wrong, but then I think of Jesus, and that stops me from doing wrong. I now can sing with all my heart (and without telling a lie), 'I love Jesus; yes, I do.'"

"The way I gave my heart to Jesus was, that after I heard you preach, I went into the inquiry-meeting, and there a young lady spoke to me, and after dear Mr. W——. And I thought of how cruel it had been of me not to have given my heart to him before, and I trusted in him, and he saved me. Pray for your little friend, ————,

"11 years old."

Here is another child's letter, written by one who attended some meetings for children in the Rev. Baptist Noel's chapel, in London.

She says, "I CAME TO JESUS BECAUSE I FOUND I WAS SUCH A SINNER."

"*May* 30, 1867.

"DEAR MR. HAMMOND,—I have been very happy ever since I came to the meetings, and I was very sorry when I found that I had not come to Jesus before; and on Sunday night I came to Jesus because I found I was such a sinner, and my teacher spoke to me and told me that I was a sinner, and I prayed that Jesus would take me for his own. I shall be here this evening, and try to bring my 'ticket.' I thank Mr. Noel for his kindness in having the chapel open so many evenings. I remain your little friend,

"Louisa ——,

"12 years old."

I will let you read one more letter, which I received from a child in London. She says, "I AM ALWAYS THINKING OF JESUS, OF

JESUS THE WAY. 47

HOW HE WAS NAILED UPON THE CROSS, AND HOW HE HAD THE CROWN OF THORNS UPON HIS HEAD."

"DEAR MR. HAMMOND,—I was at your meeting on Sunday night, and I did cry very much to think that I was a sinner; but when my teacher told me that Jesus would save me if I prayed to God to forgive me, I did not cry so much. And now I think that Jesus has taken me just as I am, and I can sing that beautiful hymn I feel like singing all the day,—

> "'My tears are wiped away,
> For Jesus is a friend of mine,
> I'll serve him every day.'

"I am always thinking of Jesus, how he was nailed upon the cross, and how he had the crown of thorns on his head, and then it makes me cry a little, but I try to bear it. I wish you were coming every night to preach, for I like it very much, and it did make me feel as if I could cry when those little children were saying such wicked words; and then a lady came over and spoke to them, and then they began to cry. Oh, I do hope they have found the Saviour. I send my best love to dear Mr. Noel and Mrs. Hammond. I'm 13 years old.

"From your truly converted friend,
"Florence ———."

Have *you* ever felt what a sinner you have been not to love the Saviour? Oh, I pray the Holy Spirit may show you what a wicked, ungrateful child you have been, not to love him who "first loved us."

I heard, not long ago, a touching story of how a mother in Scotland died to save the life of her child.

One very cold day in winter, she was obliged to cross a mountain with her little baby-boy in her arms. When she got to the top of the mountain, she became very cold, and began to fear that she and her little babe would freeze to death; but she resolved to take some of the clothing from herself, and wrap it around her child, and save his life. So she folded her shawl all around her infant, then she laid him out of the wind in the cleft of the rock. The next morning she was found *dead* near by, but the babe in the cleft of the rock was quite warm and well.

When that child grew up he must have loved that mother very much, for he knew how she had died to save his life. He could not remember her face, for he was too young when she died; but he loved her, and was not ashamed of her, though she was a poor woman. If he had been, I think the boys in Scotland would have felt like taking him to some high mountain, and leaving him there to freeze to death.

One day, many years after, a minister was relating this story, when a soldier came forward, and with tears in his eyes, said, "That was my mother, she died to save my life, she hid me in the cleft of the rock. I love her; but I can never tell how much I love my Saviour, who, when I was in danger of dying 'the second death,' said to me, '*I will put thee in the cleft of the rock, and will cover thee.*'"

"Rock of ages, cleft for me,
Let me hide myself in thee."

That soldier loved his mother, but he felt that Jesus had done far more for him than his mother, and no doubt he loved Christ more than he did his mother.

Now, my dear child, what are you going to do about giving your heart to Jesus? You are a guilty sinner, if you have not come to Jesus. You are in danger of being lost for ever. Christ has suffered on the cross that you might be forgiven. The Holy Spirit is ready to help you to trust in him, and Jesus is ready to save you. Will you come to him just now? Oh, then fall down before him, and come to him while offering this

Child's Prayer.

Dear Saviour, I come to thee, a poor, lost sinner. Though I am but a child, I know I am very wicked; I have never loved thee. I have sometimes *thought* that I loved thee, but now I fear that I have never done so. I now wish to love thee. Thou hast loved me more than any friend on earth ever loved me. Show me, O God, how that because thy dear Son has died for sinners, I may now be saved, and be made fit for heaven. Holy Spirit, help me to cling to Jesus. May I see that it is because he has died " the just for the unjust," that I can be treated by God as if I had never sinned. Help me to have true faith in Jesus, so that I can say, " Being justified by faith, we have peace with God, through our Lord Jesus Christ," in whose name I pray. *Amen.*

JESUS THE WAY.

Jesus, thou hast loved me more
I would now thy name adore,
   Than that mother loved her child;
   I would serve thee all the while;
In thy pierced, wounded side,
Help me now with faith to hide.

Now I see that all my tears
   Will not cleanse my soul from sin;
Thou alone canst quell my fears,
   Thou canst make me pure within;
Thou the Rock of ages art,
Only thou canst change my heart.

To thy work alone, I'll cling,
   While I live and when I die;
Of thy finished work I'll sing,
   Here on earth and in the sky;
Even there my song shall be,
"*Rock of ages, cleft for me.*"

CHAPTER IV.

TO JERUSALEM.

I have told you in the other chapters in this book, a little about our visit to Palestine. I often thought when we were riding through that country, that I should love to write a full account of it for children, that they might understand the Bible better, and be more interested in it. But I have not attempted it in this book, because my great object has been to lead my little readers to trust in Jesus, and be saved.

If you will look upon a map of Palestine, you may be interested in at least learning the names of some of the places through which we passed on our journey to Jerusalem, the Dead Sea, and to Hebron.

In the last chapter you know we spoke of Sarepta, which is a few miles south of Sidon. The next night our tents were pitched near the walls of Tyre, where King Hiram, the friend of Solomon, lived three thousand years ago. We saw scattered along the beach the ruins and pillars of the temple of that city, which, at the command of God, was destroyed for its wickedness. We read the twenty-third chapter of Isaiah, and the twenty-eighth chapter of Ezekiel. There we saw that God had done just what he said: "They shall lay thy stones, and thy timber, and thy dust in the midst of the water." (Ezek. xxvi. 12).

From Tyre, we turned to the east, passing the tomb of Hiram, to Tibnin, where we spent the night. On our way we stopped at Kanah, under an olive-tree, to lunch. It was not long before all the children in the village were gathered around us. We thought it a good time to have a children's meeting, and to tell them about Jesus, "THE CHILD'S GUIDE TO HEAVEN." Our dragoman, who could speak Arabic, was the interpreter. After singing to them an American hymn, we told them that we had come five thousand miles to see the land where Jesus lived, and that we were going to Jerusalem to see the place where he died on the cross for us. They listened to every word that we said. We prayed for them that they might trust in Christ and be saved.

At Tibnin we had another meeting for children. From thence we passed over a high hill, or mountain, across the Jordan to Cæsarea Philippi (Matt. xvi. 13). It is at the foot of Mount Hermon, and though it was warm in the valley, the top of that mountain, nearly two miles high, was covered with snow.

Then we turned southward, and journeyed on, day after day, through many interesting places which are mentioned in the Bible. On we passed through Kedesh, one of the cities of refuge, to Safed, "the city set upon a hill," where we spent the night, and got our first view of the beautiful sea of Galilee.

We spent several days very pleasantly in visiting the ruins of the cities which once stood upon the shores of that lovely lake, where our Saviour spent so much time during his ministry upon earth.

We attempted to sail across the lake, but a terrrible storm overtook us, and we came very near losing our lives; but like the disciples of old upon that same sea, we prayed to Jesus, "Master, carest thou not that we we perish? and he arose and rebuked the wind, and said unto the sea, Peace, be still, and the wind ceased, and there was a great calm."

Jesus the Way. SEA OF GALILEE.

JESUS THE WAY.

We started for Bethsaida,
   On board a little crazy ship;
The distance seemed not very far,
   And o er the waves we hoped to skip.

When we were out a little way,
   The doctor of our party said,
"I hope we'll have a storm to-day,"
   And turned to his book and read.

Soon from Mount Hermon's lofty height,
   And from the hills of Naphtali,
Fierce, angry clouds burst on our sight,
   And swept the waves of Galilee.

Its placid waters then were tossed
   In foaming billows all around;
In vain we wished the sea were crossed,
   And we were on the solid ground.

The billows rolled, the winds were high,
   And every heart grew anxious then;
We prayed, "O Saviour, come thou nigh,
   And still the waters once again."

The Saviour heard our pleading cry,
   And quickly stilled our wild alarm
He to our rescue soon did fly,
   And suddenly the sea was calm.

'T was then we felt the Saviour near,
   As did his followers, on that sea;
He from our hearts had banished fear,
   And quelled the waves of Galilee.

> Dear Saviour, may we ever feel
> That thou art never far away,
> But that wherever we may kneel,
> There thou art near us as we pray.

These lines came to my mind, and I jotted them down after the wind had ceased, as we were returning in our boat to Tiberias.

Leaving that beautiful valley, we passed to the top of Mount Hattin, where it is supposed Christ's "Sermon on the Mount" was preached, and from thence through Cana of Galilee to Nazareth. We spent three days in wandering about that lovely spot, where our Saviour passed thirty years of his life.

After going to the top of Mount Tabor, we rode by Nain, where Jesus raised the young man to life (Luke vii. 11-15), and to Shunem, where, in answer to the prayer of the prophet Elisha, the sun-stricken boy was made to live again (II. Kings iv. 18-37).

On we hastened, through Jezreel, where King Ahab lived; through Dothan, where Joseph was sold by his brethren; through

Jesus the Way.   JERUSALEM.

JESUS THE WAY.

Samaria, where Philip preached until "there was great joy in that city" (Acts viii. 8); through Shechem, where we saw the tomb of Joseph, and Jacob's well. After going to the top of Mount Gerizim, we bade adieu to the vale of Shechem, and passed on through Shiloh, where little Samuel lived when the Lord called him (I. Sam. iii. 4); and to Bethel, where Jacob saw in a dream the ladder "which reached to heaven" (Gen. xxviii. 12).

Finally, we looked upon the city which we wished to see more than any other city in the whole world. I need not tell you it was JERUSALEM. It was on the first day of December, 1866, when it first burst upon our view from Mount Scopus.

The gentlemen of our party took off their hats, and we stood gazing upon it in silence. The tears filled my eyes as I thought of how it was on Calvary, by the side of the ancient walls of that city, that Jesus died for me.

Oh, how thankful we were that God had spared our lives to see that holy city!

As soon as we reached our hotel, we asked to be shown the place where Jesus was crucified. We were quickly led to the spot where many suppose he was lifted up on the cross, "that we should not perish, but have everlasting life." I cannot tell you how I felt my heart going out in fresh love to Jesus as I stood there. By my side I noticed a little boy kneeling in prayer. He looked very solemn and earnest. He was about eight years of age. I think his father had brought him all the way from Italy. If I could have spoken his language, I should have loved to talk with the little fellow about Jesus, the "child's Guide to heaven." Many ignorant people think that because they have been to Jerusalem they are sure of heaven; but this is a great mistake. I hope that little boy did not make such a mistake.

In Jerusalem we found a great many

JESUS THE WAY.

people from all parts of the world, who had come thousands of miles to see "the place where he was crucified." It is to "*the place where he was crucified*" that I want *you* to come before you finish this chapter. With the eye of faith I wish you to see Jesus on the cross, bleeding and dying for you. 'Tis my earnest prayer that you may be able to say, in the words of this little hymn which I wrote for the children in America,

> Jesus from his throne on high
> Came into this world to die;
> That I might from sin be free,
> Bled and died upon the tree.
>
> I can see him, even now,
> With his pierced, thorn-clad brow,
> Agonizing on the tree.
> Oh, what love! and all for me.
>
> Now I feel this heart of stone
> Drawn to love God's only Son,
> "Lifted up" on Calvary,
> Suffering shame and death for me.
>
> Jesus, take this heart of mine;
> Make it pure and wholly thine;

> Thou hast bled and died for me;
> I will henceforth live for thee.

As I went thousands of miles to see the city where Jesus was crucified, I am sure you will be anxious to hear all you can about that precious Saviour who was there "wounded for our transgressions."

I have been praying very earnestly that God would help me so to write to you in this chapter, of the finished work of Christ, that you may deeply feel that he really died a dreadful death on the cross that you might be saved.

You have heard about Jesus ever since you can remember, but yet, perhaps, you do not understand why he came from his home in heaven down into this wicked world. Let me try and tell you all about it; and I hope at the same time you will be asking God to help you, by his Holy Spirit, to trust in Jesus. God has told us in his Book, that if we would obey all his good laws, never think a wrong thought, nor speak a wrong word, nor do a wrong act, that we should be happy here, and, at last, live for ever in the mansions in heaven. He also told us that if we broke any of his just laws, that he should have to punish us; that we should have many tears and sorrows here, and, at last, be shut out of heaven for ever.

God said to our first parents, to try them, that if they broke but one of his commands, that they should "surely die" (Gen. ii. 17). But they disbelieved God, and believed Satan, the "father of lies," who said to them, "Ye shall not surely die" (Gen. iii. 3). They were then cast out of the garden of Eden, and the curse of God was upon them; and all who have lived since that sad day, have, like Adam and Eve, disobeyed God. Yes, "all have sinned" (Rom. iii. 23). Every little child has sinned. As soon as a child is old enough to know right from wrong, it is old enough to love God, whose words are, "Son, give me thine heart."

Now, if a little child does not love God, he has broken one of God's laws, and how can he be saved? That was the great question in heaven. How can a world of sinners be saved? Then it was that God's own Son, the Lord Jesus Christ, offered himself for us as a ransom; and God, who always wished to save every sinner if possible, said, "*Deliver him from going down to the pit, I have found a ransom.*"

He might have left us to perish, but " God so loved the world that he gave his only begotten Son, that whosoever believeth in him should not perish, but have everlasting life." (John iii. 16). At the appointed time Jesus came into the world, and took upon himself our nature. Though he was God, he became also a man, that he might be able to sympathize with us. As a man he obeyed the law of God perfectly. He never committed one sin: "He was holy, harmless, undefiled."

Thirty years he lived at Nazareth. "He was a man of sorrows, and acquainted with grief." "Though he was rich, yet for our sakes he became poor." When we were in Nazareth, we saw the "brow of the hill," where we were told his town's-people tried to thrust him down and kill him. They were angry with him because he preached to them so plainly. They hated him without a cause. He used to open the eyes of the blind, heal the sick, and raise the dead. In Bethany he called Lazarus back to life, and brought him out of the tomb. My wife and I went to see the stone tomb, where we were told Lazarus lay "in the grave four days."

After Jesus had wrought many miracles, and thus shown that he was not a mere man, the time came for him to die upon the cross.

Between Jerusalem and the mount of Olives was the garden of Gethsemane, where

Jesus went the night before he was crucified. While thinking of how much he must suffer if he would save us, and while in prayer to God, "His sweat was as it were great drops of blood falling down to the ground" (Luke xxii. 44). While he was in that garden with his disciples, a multitude took him and brought him into the house of the high-priest; "and the men that held Jesus mocked him, and smote him, and when they had blindfolded him, they struck him on the face, and asked him, saying, Prophesy, who is it that smote thee?" (Luke xxii. 63, 64.)

But the Jews had no power to put Jesus to death, and so "the whole multitude arose and led him unto Pilate" (Luke xxiii. 1). But Pilate said, "I find no fault in this man." He was afraid to give orders to have him crucified. He knew very well that it was because the people hated him that they wished to get rid of him; and so, when he heard that Jesus' home had been in Galilee,

JESUS THE WAY.

he sent him to Herod, who was the governor of that district. But "Herod with his men of war set him at nought, and mocked him, and arrayed him in a gorgeous robe, and sent him again to Pilate" (Luke xxiii. 11). But his wife sent unto him, saying, "Have thou nothing to do with that just man, for I have suffered many things this day in a dream because of him" (Matt. xxvii. 19). But Pilate had no love for Jesus, "he feared the people." He was afraid he should lose his office if he did not seek to please them; yet he sought in several ways to save Jesus from crucifixion. He thought that it might satisfy the "chief priests and the rulers of the people," if he should cause Jesus to be scourged; and so he said to them, "I will chastise him and release him." He thought when they saw his back all covered with blood it would satisfy them; "Pilate, therefore, took Jesus and scourged him;" and to insult him still more, "the soldiers platted a crown of thorns and put it on his head, and they put on him a purple robe, and said, Hail! King of the Jews, and they smote him with their hands,"—when his back was all bleeding, and the crimson drops trickling down his face, from the crown of thorns pressed down into his brow, and his "face marred more than the face of any man,"— when he had been buffetted with clenched fists, —then Pilate brought him forth before the cruel murderers, and said, "Behold the man." "I find no fault in him." But no, they were not satisfied. "They cried out, Crucify him! crucify him! away with him! crucify him." "Then delivered he him therefore unto them to be crucified" (John xix. 16, 17). "He, bearing his cross, went forth into a place of a skull, where they crucified him." For more than three hours Jesus hung upon the cross, with the nails driven through his hands and through his feet. The sun refused to shine upon that awful deed. And when he cried, "IT IS FINISHED," "the earth did quake, and the rocks rent," as if they seemed to sympathise with the dying Saviour.

I wish I could tell you some of the feelings we had while visiting those places where our Saviour suffered so much during his last few hours on earth. We walked from the garden of Gethsemane to the place where Pilate's hall once stood, and then along the road where it is said Jesus bore the cross to Calvary. It is now called "The Sorrowful Way." Our guide showed us the place where tradition says he fell beneath the heavy cross.

We saw numbers of people from all parts of the world slowly walking along that sorrowful way to the place where, it is generally believed, Jesus "bare our sins in his own body on the tree." As we followed them, we could not but think of Jesus all the time. When we came near the place where many think he was crucified, these words came to my mind,

> 'T was for me that Jesus bled
>   On the cruel tree;
> There he bowed his thorn-clad head:
>   Oh, what agony!
>
> 'T was my sin that nailed him there,
>   Mine that shed his blood,
> Mine that pierced the bleeding side
>   Of the Son of God!

As I walked about those places where Jesus suffered so much for us, I could not keep the tears from my eyes. In the garden of Gethsemane, my wife and I wept and prayed together. I felt that I wished to love the dear Saviour more, and to work for him more earnestly, and never to weary in his service. I often thought of those words in Eph. v. 2, "CHRIST ALSO HATH LOVED US, AND HATH GIVEN HIMSELF FOR US AN OFFERING AND A SACRIFICE TO GOD."

On the cross, you know, he cried, "IT IS FINISHED." Yes then he "finished" all that was needful for a world's salvation.

Though his body was put into the grave, God showed that he accepted the sacrifice his Son had made, by raising him from the tomb after three days. And now God offers pardon to all that will come and confess their sins, and believe in Jesus. His words to all guilty sinners are, "BELIEVE ON THE LORD JESUS CHRIST, AND THOU SHALT BE SAVED."

Now, my dear child, I hope you have understood these last very important pages which you have just read.

You remember that I told you that I wept, when in Jerusalem, to think that I had not loved the Saviour more, and done more for him. Yet I *knew* that I loved him a *great deal*, for I had worked for him many, many years. But how is it with *you*, my dear little one? Have you ever really loved Jesus at all? Can it be that you have read these words from the Bible about the torture and sufferings of

Christ for us, and yet have never thanked him for it?

What a hard, wicked heart you must have! I should think you would go to God at once and ask him, for Jesus' sake, to forgive you all your sins, and to give you a new heart; for he says, "A new heart also will I give you, and a new spirit will I put within you" (Ezek. xxxvi. 26).

If some friend on earth had died to save your body from death, you would love his very name.

It is said that once, when a fierce war was raging, ten men were condemned to be shot. A little before the time came when they were to suffer death, a friend of one of them came to him, and said, "I will die for you."

"Why do you offer to die for me?"

"Because I love you, I am willing to be shot in your place. You have a wife and children, I have none. After I am shot, you can go home and take care of them."

The officers in power gave their consent, and that kind soldier died for his friend, and the soldier condemned to be shot was freely pardoned *for his friend's sake* who died for him.

Do you think that soldier loved the very name of that soldier who died for him? Do you think he was ever ashamed to speak of him? Oh no, he told his children when he got home, all about it. Perhaps his little boy said,

"Papa, that soldier, who died for you was your saviour, was he not? He saved you from that awful death. Though I never saw him, I shall always love him. If I ever find any of his friends, I shall be very kind to them."

'Twas not so very strange that one *friend* should die for another; but Christ died for his *enemies*. You will see this if you look in Romans v. 7-10. Yes, when you were condemned to die "the second death," and to be forever shut out from heaven, Christ suffered all those tortures, and that dreadful death of which you have read, that you might be forgiven and saved. It was not in his body that he suffered merely; it was *soul-suffering* that made the bloody sweat stand upon his brow. In the garden, that dreadful night before he was crucified, he exclaimed, "My soul is exceeding sorrowful, even unto death" (Mark xiv. 34). He knew that if he gave himself up to be "made sin for us" (II. Cor. v. 21); that is, to be treated as a sinner in our stead, that even his heavenly Father would turn his face from him when he hung bleeding on the cross.

And so it was; for you know that when his disciples had all forsaken him, and wicked men were reviling him, saying, "He saved others, himself he cannot save" (Luke xxvii. 42); then it was he cried out in agony, *"My God, my God, why hast thou forsaken me?"*

JESUS THE WAY.

> Think how the holy Saviour bled
>   Upon the cruel tree;
> Ask what means that doleful cry
>   Of bitter agony.
>
> 'T was not because the piercing nails
>   His hands and feet had torn;
> 'T was not because his blessed brow
>   Had felt the wreathèd thorn.
>
> But deeper sorrows far than these,
>   The blessed Saviour knew;
> For ah! his soul was tasting then
>   The death to sinners due.
>
> 'T was love, 't was love, to ruined man,
>   Whose sin he deigned to bear,
> That sinners, through his death of shame,
>   Eternal life might share.

Yes, my dear child, it was for your sake and my sake that Jesus was forsaken on the cross. I am sure that I love him for it, and what an ungrateful heart you must have if you do not love him too!

If you will only go to him as you are, he will forgive you, and you will feel as a little girl did whom I knew in London, when she first trusted in him. She came to some meetings in one of the churches where God was pouring out his spirit, and heard the story of Christ's sufferings for us. She felt sorry that she had not loved him, and she repented of this and her other sins, and gave herself up to the dear Saviour. He received her as he always does children who come thus to him, and from that moment she began to live a new life. She felt that she was in a new world. She then knew what our Saviour meant when he said to Nicodemus, "Verily, verily, I say unto thee except a man be born again, he cannot see the kingdom of God" (John iii. 3). 'Twas the *new birthday* of her soul when she trusted in Jesus.

A few days after, a friend of hers handed me these lines, expressive of this little girl's joyous feelings, which I am sure you will like to read.

MY NEW BIRTHDAY.

Shall I tell you of a birthday,
I had a few weeks past,

JESUS THE WAY.

The joy of which will ever stay
    When time itself has passed?

There was a good man preaching,
    Not very far away
From where I lived, and so I thought
    I'd hear him, too, one day.

So I and several others,
    Were taken by a friend,
To hear of Christ the Saviour,
    Who loved us without end.

I'd heard of Jesus Christ before,
    When at the Sunday-school;
But never thought he died for *me*,
    That I might be made whole.

But on that self-same evening,
    I've mentioned once before,
I saw so very clearly
    That *Jesus is the Door*.

When I had heard the story
    Of Christ, the bleeding Lamb
I just at once believed it,
    And holy joy then came.

And I've been very happy,
    Since that glad, joyful day,
When I began to trust in Christ,
    And first began to pray.

And you may have a birthday,
    If you to Christ will come,

> He will at once receive you,
>   And guide you to your home.
>
> I cannot tell you half the pain
>   He suffered on the tree;
> By wicked men was crucified,
>   That he might see us free.

You may like to read a letter from a little boy in one of the islands of the English Channel. He was only seven years old when he wrote it. I have seen his parents, who are Christians, and they told me that he really seems to have a new heart. I have seen him several times since he wrote the letter, and he told me he still loved the Saviour. Some of the words are badly spelled, but no matter, you can understand what he says.

"DEAR SIR,

"I am very thankful to you for helping me when I was in great trouble about my sins. But now I see that Jesus christ Died on the cross to save me a sinner. I love to sing that little hymn,—

> Jesus from his throne on high
> Came into this world to die;
> That from sin I might be free,
> Bled and died upon the tree,
>> Yes, Jesus loves me; yes, Jesus loves me;
>> Yes, Jesus loves me; the Bible tells me so.

I am very much composed since I came to your meetings, I like to come to your meetings very much. I would Be very much oblighed to you if you would pray for me, and I will pray for you when I am a man, if ever I be one. I should like to Be a missionary, and go and teach the little black boys about Jesus.

"Mother and father tells me that I can find every thing in the Bible, and I mean to read it if I am spared.

>"Your little friend,
>> "Edward B———,
>>> "7 years old."

Here is another letter from a child in Guernsey. I think you will feel that the little writer knows what it is to trust in Jesus, It is my prayer that you, too, may be able to say,—

"I FELT MY WEIGHT OF SIN WAS GONE, AND NOW I AM HAPPY IN THE LORD."

"GUERNSEY *September 6th* 1867.
"DEAR SIR

"I want to tell you how i found Jesus I went to one of your meetings 2 weeks ago and i had been seeking Jesus a long time and i felt determined that i would not leave the chapel till I had given my heart to god i felt that I was a great sinner I wanted some one to talk to me about the saviour and i was afraid that no one would come and talk to me but Mrs. Pring came and spoke to me and i went down in the vestry with her and Mr. Pring prayed with me and *i felt my weight of sin was gone and now I am happy in the Lord* I want to work for Jesus All my life time that when i die that I might meet you in heaven where we shall sing the praises of the Lord and reign with him for evermore please do not forget your little friend in your prayers

"' Do you love Jesus I was asked
   With shame I answered no
Oh what a sinner i have been
   To treat my saviour so

But now of him I'm not ashamed
   Who bore my load of guilt
I love I love his blessed name
   For me his Blood was spilt

I love to sing that little hymn
   Of Jesus paid it all
To think that I've rejected him
   Makes Tears begin to fall'

" Dear Sir i prayed Me and another little girl for a little boy i knew and i believe god have answered our prayer for he told me he had to go to his room and pray to god to wash away his sin and he rose with a light and happy heart thank God for it all.

  "I remain your affectionate friend,
                    " ALICE."

Now, my dear little child, what are you going to do about coming to Jesus? If you do not come to him before you finish this chapter, we must part company, for the next chapter is for little Christians. I think that after what you have read in this book, you understand how it is that God can forgive us for Christ's sake.

I have tried to lift up Jesus by these simple stories and illustrations, so that you might with the eye of faith see him, and hear him saying to you, "Look unto me and be ye saved" (Isa. xlv. 22). He has said also, and "I, if I be lifted up, will draw all men unto me" (John xii. 32). In the language in which the Bible was first written, the word *"men"* was left out, so that it read, and "I, if I be lifted up, will draw *all* unto me." Yes, when little children see him bleeding on the cross for them, and hear him saying, "Suffer little children to come unto me," how can they but flee to his open arms?

Oh then, come to him just now with this

Child's Prayer.

Dear Saviour, thou hast been very kind to die for sinful children like me, but I have been very wicked not to love thee. Other children have loved thee, but I have often been ashamed of thee. I come and confess this my sin, and all my sins; I wish to forsake them and live for thee, who hast done so much for me. Please to open my blind eyes, that I may see thee as thou art, the Friend and Saviour of little children, "the chiefest among ten thousand," and the One altogether lovely. Please to give me a new heart, so that I shall love thee, and love to pray to thee, and love the Bible, and thy dear people. I give myself to thee, 'tis all that I can do. Strengthen me to work for thee, and to try to bring others to thee. Holy Spirit, help me to believe in the Lord Jesus Christ with all my heart.

Hear this, my prayer, O God, for Jesus' sake. Amen.

> Though I never see the place
>   Where, dear Saviour, thou didst die,
> Yet I oft may see thy face,
>   When with faith to thee I fly.
>
> Pleasant it indeed would be
>   Could I to that city go,
> Where upon dark Calvary,
>   Thou didst die so long ago.
>
> Need I go so far away?
>   No, for thou art very near;
> Thou wilt hear me if I pray,
>   Thou wilt drive away my fear
>
> Jesus, now I come to thee,
>   Show me, Lord, thy pierced brow,
> Speaking of thy love to me,
>   Help me come to thee just now.

CHAPTER V.

VISIT TO CAPERNAUM.

IF you have read carefully thus far in this little book, and have obeyed its teaching, I can but hope that you have been enabled, by the help of God's Spirit, to trust in Jesus. If you have really repented of your sins, and believed in him, then God, for his sake, has given you a new heart, and you are now a Christian.

As I have traveled about in different countries, I have found many little children who truly love the Saviour; I have also talked with many who began to love him when they were so young that they could not remember the time when their hearts were first filled with his love.

A few weeks ago I stood by the grave of "the mother of the Wesleys," and I remembered that she was one of those who gave her heart to Christ when she was too young to remember it. 'Tis not strange that she should have done so. Can you tell me, my dear child, when you first began to love your mother? I know you cannot. But if when you were very little, only three or four years of age, you had been told that Jesus had loved you far more than your mother had, and that he had done far more for you, would you not have loved him? So you see it is not strange that very young children should come to him, and love him, and thank him for his goodness in dying for them.

Besides these children who so early love the Saviour, I know of many under twelve years of age, who seem truly to have given their hearts to God; and the friends of some of them have told me, that they were showing, by their happy and obedient lives, that God had forgiven them all their sins.

Now the words in this chapter are for such little ones who are true Christians. If you are one of those who truly love Jesus, then you will understand what I am about to say; and I pray that it may help you to cling closer to Jesus, and seek to win others to him. I know of but few books for little Christians. There are many good books for children, yet scarcely any specially for those who have been converted from their sins.

Before I talk to you about what it is to be a Christian, I wish to tell you about what thoughts I had when visiting the ruins of Capernaum on the shores of the sea of Galilee.

One beautiful afternoon in November, 1866, when it was as warm as summer in America, we left our tents at Tiberias, on the south-western shore of the lake, and galloped along upon our fleet horses, by

Magdala, where Mary Magdalene once lived, and along the sandy beach where our Saviour so often preached when on earth; till finally we came to a great pile of stones and ruins on the northern shore of the lake. There our guide told us was the place where Capernaum once stood. From our books we learned that he was no doubt correct.

He first took us to the ruins of a beautiful synagogue, recently excavated by Professor Wilson. We felt quite sure that Jesus had often trodden upon that very marble pavement. We were very glad to get off our horses to go down among the broken marble columns, and to place our feet upon that same pavement. I was more interested in the ruins of Capernaum than of any other of the cities which we saw by the sea of Galilee. I will tell you the reason.

Jesus, you know, lived at Nazareth till he was thirty years of age. One day, when he was preaching a sermon in their synagogue, they "were filled with wrath," "and rose up to thrust him out of the city, and led him unto the brow of the hill whereon their city was built, that they might cast him down headlong." But he escaped from them, "and came down to Capernaum," which he adopted as "his own city." No wonder that I felt a deep interest in the ruins of *that city?* How I wished that those broken columns of that old synagogue could speak. But they answered none of my questions, so I turned to the precious Bible, and read all I could about what Jesus did and said in "his own city." Nothing interested me more than the account of his raising to life Jairus's "little daughter," who "was of the age of twelve years." We read the different accounts in Matthew xi., Mark v., and Luke viii., and thought a great deal about it.

This little child, you know, was the daughter of a good man, who was "a ruler of the synagogue." He loved her very much, for she was " his only daughter." But she was taken ill, and she grew worse and worse, till one day "she lay a-dying." Then it was her father thought of Jesus, who was in the city, and when he found him, " he besought him greatly," saying, " My little daughter lieth at the point of death. I pray thee come and lay thy hands on her, that she may be healed, and she shall live." Jesus at once " went with him;" but much people followed him, and thronged him, so that he could not get along very fast. Among the crowd was a poor woman, who had " had an issue of blood for twelve years;" and her words were, " If I may but touch the hem of his garment I shall be made whole." While he lingered for a little to tell this woman that her faith had saved her, " there came from the ruler of the synagogue's house certain which said, Thy daughter is dead: why troublest thou the Master?" But Jesus heard their words, and said, " Be not afraid, only believe."

On he went to the house, and there he found the friends weeping very bitterly, for they knew the child was dead. But Jesus said to her, "*Maid, arise.* And her spirit came again, and she rose up straightway; and he commanded to give her meat."

Now how do you think this little girl felt towards the dear Saviour? Whenever he came home from visits in the country to "his own city," do you not think she was always very glad to see him? Very likely she often ran to meet him, and put her little hand in his, and told him how much she loved him; and do you not suppose she told her little friends about her *Saviour?* Oh yes, she must have told them all about him, and how he raised her to life.

Now you may wonder why I have spent so much time in telling you about Jarius's "little daughter." I will tell you.

In the second chapter of Ephesians, are these words, "And you hath he quickened who were dead in trespasses and sins." These words Paul wrote to the people of Ephesus who had, as lost sinners, believed in Jesus, and so were raised from the grave of sin, and made to live a new life. All who are not Christians, are "dead in trespasses and sins." Every child that does not love Jesus, is in a sense "dead." It has no desire for the rich food in God's word.

What would you have thought if, when Jarius's daughter was dead, they had brought in something for her to eat? Those who were standing by her bed would have said, "She is dead, she cannot eat any more." But after Jesus had raised her to life, he commanded to give her meat.

Just so have I seen children who had rather sit and play, or fall asleep, when good men have offered them the *Bread of Heaven*. Why did they behave in this way? Ah! they were *dead*. And I have seen those same children, after they had been raised to newness of life, sitting quietly and listening to the Bible when it was read, as if they were feeding upon its precious truths.

Do you, my dear children, love the Bible? Can you say that "It is sweeter also than honey and the honeycomb?" Then this is one sign that you have begun to live a new life. It is called in the Bible an *everlasting life,* because it will never end. "He that believeth on the Son hath everlasting life," "is passed from death unto life."

If you are living this new life of faith in Jesus, you will need food every day. The meat that was given to Jarius's daughter did not satisfy her all her life. Every day she needed something to eat. So it is with you. That was the reason our Saviour taught us to pray, "Give us this day our daily bread."

One day in Newark, New Jersey, I received two hundred and ten letters from children, who said they had become Christians. Most of them were under twelve years of age. They told how it was that Jesus had raised them to life. Many of them used words like these, "One reason why I think I am a Christian, is because *I love the Bible* now in a way I never did before; I can understand it a great deal better." It was nearly four years ago that those letters were written, and I have seen many of those children since; I have been glad to find that they loved the Bible more and more. I hope it will be so with you. I am almost sure it will be, if you have truly been converted.

Here is another thing I wish you to think about. How do you suppose that little girl in Capernaum felt toward Jesus after he had called her back to life again? "Oh!" you say, "I know she loved him very much." Yes, I have no doubt of it; whenever she heard him preach, how still she must have sat to drink in every word he spake. Now, if you are a Christian, you will love the Saviour, and wish to do all you can to please him.

Here is a letter which a little girl in London wrote me a few months ago. She is one year younger than was Jarius's daughter; she says, "I FELT VERY SORRY TO THINK THAT I HAD BEEN SO WICKED NOT TO LOVE JESUS."

"DEAR SIR,—

"I wished to write and tell you how very happy I feel since I have loved the dear Jesus. Last Tuesday evening I came to the Scotch Church, and heard you speak about Jesus. I felt very sorry to think I had been so wicked, not to love Jesus, who had suffered so much and died for me. I could not help crying; but a kind gentleman talked to me, and now I am sure that I love Jesus, and he loves me. Please to pray for me, that I may always love him, and that my sister may love him too. I am eleven years old. I am, your ever grateful,

"ALICE.

"If ye love me keep my commandments."

Here is another letter from a child, about the same age as Jairus's daughter. She writes as if Jesus had raised her from the tomb of sin. Have you ever felt as she did when she said, "I WEPT VERY MUCH TO THINK HOW WICKED I HAD BEEN NEVER TO THANK OR LOVE HIM FOR TWELVE YEARS"?

"Dear Mr. Hammond,—

"I was very much impressed with your meetings. I came on Sunday night, not thinking of what I was going to hear. I was very inattentive until one sentence caught my ear, and that was, 'and you have never thanked him.' I listened and heard you tell how Jesus died for us on the cross. That went to my heart like an arrow. I wept very much to think *how wicked I had been never to thank or love him for twelve years and six months.* I felt that it was a great many years to live without loving Jesus. A lady spoke to me, and so did dear Mr. Noel. I went away that night rejoicing.

"Your little friend,
"————.

"Just twelve years and six months old."

"I BELIEVE I HAVE GOT HOLD OF THE FIRST LINK OF THE GOLDEN CHAIN."

These were the words of a dear girl in London, who had been attending some children's meetings, where a number of little ones had just begun to trust in him who is the "*child's Guide to heaven.*" I will let you read a part of her letter. "I believe I have got hold of the first link of the golden chain, that you told us about; for I love Jesus now, and I am sorry I did not before. How kind the Saviour was to die for our sins. I seemed to hear him say, 'Come unto me, and I will take you as you are, in all your sins, and make you happy forever.' And so he has taken my sins all away, and has given me a new heart, and now I am very happy.

"I love to sing,—

> "Now I have found a Friend,
> Jesus is mine;
> His love shall never end,
> Jesus is mine.

"Now I love my teacher very much. I hope that I shall get hold of the last link of the golden chain when I die

"Your little friend,

"————."

Let me tell about that golden chain of which she speaks. It is very wonderful. It reaches all the way from earth to heaven, and yet it has only five links in it. But if you have hold of the first link you will get hold of the last one by-and-by.

It may be in one week, or not till seventy years have passed away. My dear mother did not reach the last link until she was seventy-three years of age. A little before that time she used to sit by my side, and pray for me while I was writing books for children. But I have known some children to get hold of the first and last link within a few weeks' time. If you have hold of this golden chain, you will not part with it for the world. Let me tell you the names of the links.

I. Jesus.—II. Holiness.—III. Usefulness.—IV. Happiness.—V. Heaven.

Do you see why the links are in this order? I will tell you. When a little child, as a lost sinner, comes to JESUS, *the first link*, and trusts in him to be saved, then God gives that child what the Bible calls "*a new heart*" (Ezek. xxxvi. 26), so that he loves the good things which he never thought of before, and hates the bad things which he loved be-before. He begins at once to be a better and holier, that is, a more perfect child. And so he lays hold of the second link, HOLINESS. He may still *sometimes* do wrong, but he will repent of it, and will ask God's forgiveness, and he will seek every day to be more and more like Jesus, who was perfectly *holy*.

Are you quite sure, my dear child, that *you* have hold of Jesus, the first link of the golden chain? then it will not be long before you will have hold of the third link, USEFULNESS.

Yes, if you sincerely love Jesus, you will obey him, and work for him. You will do all you can to lead others to him. You will pray for them, and seek to show them, by your example, that religion is something for *this* world, as well as for the world to come. They will see that Jesus helps you to overcome a bad temper, and to be more obedient, amiable, and gentle. Thus you will soon find that you have hold of the fourth link, HAPPINESS. Yes, you will at times feel very happy. I have seen hundreds of children weeping to think they had not hold of Jesus with the hand of faith, and after a few days I have seen most of them filled with joy, and heard them singing,—

> "I feel like singing all the time,
>   My tears are wiped away;
> For Jesus is a Friend of mine,
>   I'll serve him every day.
>   Singing, Glory, glory,
>   Glory be to God on high.
>
> "When on the cross my Lord I saw,
>   Nailed there by sins of mine,
> Fast fell the burning tears: but now
>   I'm singing all the time.
>
> "When fierce temptations try my heart,
>   I'll sing, 'Jesus is mine;'
> And so, though tears at times may start,
>   I'm singing all the time.
>
> "Oh, happy little singing one,
>   What music is like thine?
> With Jesus as thy Life and Sun,
>   Go singing all the time.
>
> "The melting story of the Lamb
>   Tell with that voice of thine,
> Till others with the glad new song
>   Go singing all the time."

I think you see how those who trust in *Jesus*, the first link, and live *holy, useful, happy* lives, are sure of *heaven* at last.

Do not think that you are any more apt to die if you become a Christian in childhood. A great many children seem to think so; but it is because, in Sunday-school books, they so often read about Christian children that die young. I have sometimes thought such books do more harm than good, for I have found that many children fear, if they become Christians, they will die young. Oh no, I think that Christian children are more apt to live long lives.

But though you may live until you are seventy years of age, if you have got hold of the *first* link of the golden chain, then by-and-by you will reach the last link, and we shall meet in heaven.

One day, in Brixton, London, I told the children about this golden chain, and more than a hundred thought they had hold of it. I wish you could have seen their happy faces. Some time afterwards, a friend wrote me,—"The dear children are holding on, or rather

Christ is holding them, and it is a most delightful privilege to talk with them.

"One little girl of twelve years said to me, 'When I cannot come to the children's weekly prayer-meetings, we have one at home. My sisters and I go into the garden, and first we ask Jesus to be with us; I pray, and then we sing, and then we pray again, and they pray after me, and so we have our little meeting.'

"The children at Brixton were so fond of talking of the 'Golden Chain,' that I wrote a few verses, with one link in each verse, to enable them to sing it. They sing it to the tune of 'The Beautiful River,' in your tune book, which we still use.

I. JESUS.

'Now with joyous hearts we're singing,
  Christ has sought us not in vain;
To our JESUS we are clinging,
  For we've found the golden chain

Chorus.—Yes, yes, we will cling to Jesus.
  The dearest link in all the golden **chain.**

Yes, yes, we will cling to Jesus,
And we shall meet in heaven.

II. HOLINESS.

Father, make thy children holy,
Since to Jesus we have come:
Let our hearts be pure and lowly,
Fitted for thy Spirit's home.

III. USEFULNESS.

Father, make thy children useful;
Let us tell thy work of grace
To some poor benighted sinners,
That they, too, may seek thy face.

IV. HAPPINESS.

Father, thou hast made us happy,
Happy in our Saviour's love;
Now we love to sing thy praises
Ere we reach our home above.

V. HEAVEN.

Father, bring us all to heaven;
Then the last link we shall gain,—
See our Saviour's face in glory,
And complete the GOLDEN CHAIN."

You see it is not enough, because you have come to Jesus, to think there is nothing more to be done. Do you remember, little Alice closed her letter with Christ's words,

"*If ye love me, keep my commandments.*" Oh then, do not neglect to pray every day, "Give us this day our daily bread;" and do not be in the habit of merely repeating prayers which you have learned, but ask for those things which you feel you need: "*Ask, and ye shall receive.*"

Our Saviour's words to you, and to all who love him, are, "When thou prayest, enter into thy closet, and when thou hast shut thy door, pray to thy Father which is in secret; and thy Father which seeth in secret shall reward thee openly" (Matt. vi. 6).

If you will study the promises in God's word you will find them as food upon which to *feed your faith*. In this way, your faith will grow stronger every day, so that you will feel encouraged to pray for very wicked people; and God will answer your prayers. I have known many children whose prayers have been answered in the conversion of parents, brothers, and sisters.

Only a few days ago I heard how God answered the prayers of a little child only *nine* years of age. She had trusted in Christ, and God had given her a praying heart. Her father was not a Christian; far from it, he was an infidel. He tried not to believe what the Bible says about our Saviour's death and sufferings for us. She was in the habit of remaining every Sunday in the Sunday-school room, after the morning service, that she might pray alone to God.

One day, when the weather was severely cold, and the wind blowing hard, her father was afraid she would not get home alone, so he set off to meet her. He met the rest of the scholars on their way home, but she was not among them. With an anxious heart he pressed his way to the schoolroom. All was still. He cautiously opened the door, and in a moment he heard the voice of his little daughter in earnest, pleading prayer. Her cry was, "O God, have mercy upon papa; show him that he is a sinner, lead him to Jesus, make him a true Christian!"

There stood the father, not knowing what to do. God at once answered her prayer. Her father felt himself a lost sinner, he walked softly to the side of his dear child, and threw his arms around her. In a few weeks, with his little daughter, he was enabled to rejoice in the love of Jesus. He saw that Jesus was what he professed to be, the Son of God, and the only Saviour for guilty sinners like himself. He is now an active Christian, doing all he can to lead others to that Saviour whom he once hated.

If you, too, have a praying heart, you will, like this little girl, find some place where you can often be alone with your Bible and with Jesus. Do you think Jairus had to urge his little daughter to speak with Jesus when he came to their city? Oh no; he had raised her to life, and she loved him. She knew he could do anything for her.

Very likely she went to him often when she was troubled. And so, if Jesus has raised you to a new life of faith and love, I am sure you will often wish to speak with him, and tell him all your wants. "CASTING ALL YOUR CARE UPON HIM, FOR HE CARETH FOR YOU."

What sweet words those are in Isaiah xl. 11, about the Good Shepherd: "HE SHALL GATHER THE LAMBS WITH HIS ARM, AND CARRY THEM IN HIS BOSOM."

Oh, then, trust in him, cling to him, study his word, work for him, join yourself to his people, and you will thus keep fast hold of HAPPINESS, the fourth link of the Golden Chain. And, finally, you will reach the last link, HEAVEN; and when once you are in that blessed place, you will feel more deeply than you can now, that Jesus was of a truth the "CHILD'S GUIDE TO HEAVEN."

THE END.

SGCB Titles for the Young

Solid Ground Christian Books is honored to be able to offer more than a dozen uncovered treasure for children and young people.

The Child's Book on the Fall by Thomas H. Gallaudet is a simple and practical exposition of the Fall of man into sin, and his only hope of salvation.

Repentance & Faith: *Explained and Illustrated for the Young* by Charles Walker, is a two in one book introducing children to the difference between true and false faith and repentance.

A Manual for the Young by Charles Bridges is an exposition of the first nine chapters of Proverbs, called by Spurgeon "the very best."

Lectures on the Bible to the Young by John Eadie is a masterful book by true Master in Israel intended to instruct and excite to a love of the Bible.

The Child at Home by John S.C. Abbott is the sequel to his popular book *The Mother at Home*. A must read for children and their parents.

My Brother's Keeper: *Letters to a Younger Brother* by J.W. Alexander contains the actual letters Alexander sent to his ten year old brother.

The Scripture Guide by J.W. Alexander is filled with page after page of information on getting the most from our Bibles. Invaluable!

Feed My Lambs: *Lectures to Children* by John Todd is drawn from actual sermons preached in Philadelphia, PA and Pittsfield, MA to the children of the church, one Sunday each month. A pure gold-mine of instruction.

Heroes of the Reformation by Richard Newton is a unique volume that introduces children and young people to the leading figures and incidents of the Reformation. Spurgeon called him, *"The Prince of preachers to the young."*

Heroes of the Early Church by Richard Newton is the sequel to the above-named volume. The very last book Newton wrote introduces all the leading figures of the early church with lessons to be learned from each figure.

The King's Highway: *Ten Commandments to the Young* by Richard Newton is a volume of Newton's sermons to children. Highly recommended!

The Life of Jesus Christ for the Young by Richard Newton is a double volume set that traces the Gospel from Genesis 3:15 to the Ascension of our Lord and the outpouring of His Spirit on the Day of Pentecost. Excellent!

The Young Lady's Guide by Harvey Newcomb will speak directly to the heart of the young women who desire to serve Christ with all their being.

The Chief End of Man by John Hall is an exposition and application of the first question of the Westminster Shorter Catechism. Full of rich illustrations.

Call us Toll Free at 1-877-666-9469
Send us an e-mail at sgcb@charter.net
Visit us on line at solid-ground-books.com

Printed in the United States
57938LVS00001B/85